SESAME STREET

Go Green with Sesame Street

REDUCE, REUSE, AND RECYCLE, OSCAR!

Mary Lindeen

Lerner Publications ◆ Minneapolis

Cooperating and sharing are an important part of *Sesame Street*—and of taking care of our planet. We all share Earth, so it's up to all of us to take care of it together. The *Go Green with Sesame Street*® books cover everything from appreciating Earth's beauty, to conserving its resources, to helping keep it clean, and more. And the familiar, furry friends from *Sesame Street* offer young readers some easy ways to help protect their planet.

Sincerely,

The Editors at Sesame Workshop

Table of Contents

Partners on the Planet

Aren't we lucky to live on Earth together, Oscar?

Earth is fine. But my trash can? Now that's a *great* place to call home!

We Can Reduce

We can work together to keep Earth clean and healthy. One way to help is to reduce what we use.

Turn off the faucet when you are done! Then you will use less water.

Turn off the lights when you're not using them. Then you use less electricity.

Trash can pile up fast.
It doesn't just disappear!

Oh dear. That is a very big pile of trash.

When we use less, we make less trash.
That helps keep Earth clean.

What are some ways to make less trash? You could eat foods that don't have wrappers.

We Can Reuse

Reusing helps keep Earth healthy too.
We reuse when we use things more
than once.

I'm going to reuse these flowers!

Elmo can use a water bottle many times!

You can donate toys you don't use anymore.
Then other kids can use them.

Hey, Slimey, do you have any toys to give away?

We can use washable plates instead of paper plates.

My lunch box is reusable.
I bring it to school every day!

We can bring reusable cloth bags
to the store instead of plastic ones.

A can could hold pens.

That's a cozy new home for those pens!

An old container could become a bird feeder.

We Can Recycle

Recycling also helps keep Earth clean.

When we recycle, we make something old into something brand-new.

Look! These chairs were made from recycled plastic!

We can recycle paper, plastic, cans, and more.
What can you recycle in your neighborhood?

Can you think of more ways to reduce, reuse, and recycle? Let's make Earth a better place for everyone!

Earth Day Every Day

April 22 is Earth Day! On Earth Day, some people turn trash into art projects. Others clean up parks and playgrounds. You can reduce, reuse, and recycle every day. That makes every day Earth Day!

Ready to Recycle

Make it easy to recycle at home!

1. Ask an adult for some extra boxes or bins.

2. Decorate the boxes.

3. Make a sign for each box. One could say "paper." Another could say "plastic," or "bottles and cans." You could even make a box for things to donate.

4. Put the bins in a safe and handy place so everyone can use them!

Glossary

donate: to give away to someone else

electricity: a form of energy. Electricity powers things such as lights and TVs.

outgrow: to get too big for something

washable: something you can wash over and over

For Benjamin, who makes today better and tomorrow brighter

Index

Photo Acknowledgments

Additional image credits: vectortatu/Shutterstock.com, throughout (background); NASA/GSFC, p. 5; Ariel Skelley/Getty Images, pp. 6, 22; Emma Gibbs /Getty Images, p. 7; Jessica Peterson/Getty Images, p. 8; Dan Brownsword/Getty Images, p. 10;Caiaimage/Trevor Adeiline/Getty Images, p. 11; cometary /Getty Images, p. 12; JAJMO/Getty Images, p. 15; Evgeniy Agarkov/Shutterstock.com, p. 16; Littlekidmoment/Shutterstock.com, p. 17; Tim Pannell/Getty Images, p. 19; Akhmad Dody Firmansyah/Shutterstock.com, p. 20; Beatrice Sirinuntananon/Getty Images, p. 21; Beth Hall/Alamy Stock Photo, p. 23; Rawpixel .com/Shutterstock.com, pp. 24, 28;Suwit Rattiwan/Shutterstock.com, p. 26; Serenethos/Shutterstock.com, p. 29; JGI/Jamie Grill/Getty Images, p. 30. Cover: vectortatu/Shutterstock.com.

Lerner Publications Company
An imprint of Lerner Publishing Group, Inc.
241 First Avenue North
Minneapolis, MN 55401 USA

For reading levels and more information, look up this title at www.lernerbooks.com.

Main body text set in Mikado.
Typeface provided by HVD.

Library of Congress Cataloging-in-Publication Data

Names: Lindeen, Mary author. | Children's Television Workshop.
Title: Reduce, reuse, and recycle, Oscar! / Mary Lindeen.
Other titles: Sesame Street (Television program)
Description: Minneapolis : Lerner Publications, [2020] | Series: Go green with Sesame Street | Includes index. | Audience: Ages: 4-8. | Audience: Grades: K to Grade 3.
Identifiers: LCCN 2019011418 (print) | LCCN 2019015682 (ebook) | ISBN 9781541572621 (library binding : alk. paper) | ISBN 9781541583122 (eb pdf)
Subjects: LCSH: Environmentalism—Juvenile literature. | Earth Day—Juvenile literature. | Oscar the Grouch (Fictitious character)—Juvenile literature.
Classification: LCC GE195.5 .L565 2020 (print) | LCC GE195.5 (ebook) | DDC 363.7—dc23

LC record available at https://lccn.loc.gov/2019011418
LC ebook record available at https://lccn.loc.gov/2019015682

Manufactured in the United States of America
1-46529-47574-7/9/2019